D1561939

Information Literacy
in an
Information Society:

A Concept for the Information Age

Christina S. Doyle

June 1994

ERIC Clearinghouse on Information & Technology
Syracuse University
Syracuse, New York
IR - 97

This publication is available from Information Resources Publications, Syracuse University, 4-194 Center for Science and Technology, Syracuse, New York 13244-4100, 1-800-464-9107 (IR-97; $8.00 plus $2.00 shipping and handling).

ISBN: 0-937597-38-4

This publication is prepared with funding from the Office of Educational Research and Improvements, U.S. Department of Education, under contract no. RR93002009. The opinions expressed in this report do not necessarily reflect the position or policies of OERI or ED.

Table of Contents

*Information literacy is the ability to access, evaluate, and use
information from a variety of sources.*

Introduction

Information is big business today. For highly developed societies like
the United States, information is the biggest business. Over seventy
percent of American workers deal with information on the job, and new
sources of print and non-print information emerge almost daily. A week-
day edition of the *New York Times* contains more printed information
than the average seventeenth century Englishman was likely to see in a
lifetime (Wurman, 1989).

This monograph, will trace the history of the development of the term
information literacy and discuss the emergence of information literacy
as a significant organizing theme for contemporary society. A number
of educational reforms calling for changes in approaches to learning
will be used to support this discussion. Reports on the National Educational Goals (1991) (also known as *America 2000* or *Goals 2000*) and
the Secretary's Commission on Achieving Necessary Skills (SCANS)
Report (1991) will be included. Recent revisions in national subject
matter standards that imply a recognition of the process skills included
in information literacy will be examined, and outcomes for measuring
information literacy in K-12 learning situations will be outlined.

Using Information

Everyone uses information whether it be as citizens, workers, problem
solvers, or lifelong learners. Traditionally, schools have provided the
setting where individuals "learn how to learn." Major learning competencies include formulating questions, accessing potential sources of
information, evaluating the information for accuracy and pertinence,
organizing the information, and finally, applying the information to answer the original questions—the last and most valuable step in the process. It is not just finding the information, but the use of it that motivates the learner.

Before they can get to the "use" step, learners need to be thoughtfully involved with the information they find, and they must connect new information with what they already know. Once they discover new information, they must put their new understanding to use in a meaningful project. Information isn't knowledge until one does something with it. A number of reports at the national level, such as the SCANS Report, *Goals 2000*, and movements, such as reform and assessment, highlight the centrality of information literacy in the learning process.

Emphasis on New Skills

Today's educational system enjoys the challenge of producing a generation of learners and workers that will be prepared for the Information Age. This challenge calls for an emphasis on new skills. In 1991, the SCANS Report, *What Work Requires of Schools* (p. xvii-xviii) listed these new skills which parallel the societal shift away from an industrial efficiency model towards an information services model that is focused on societal effectiveness. The abilities to read, write, and compute are still important, but they are not enough. Everyone must be able to think critically, to use computers and other information technologies competently, to work with others productively, and to access and use information. Information literacy is a thematic synthesis of the skills that individuals will need to live in the Information Age.

In the last decade a variety of "literacies" have been proposed, including cultural, computer, scientific, technical, global, and mathematical. All of these literacies focus on a compartmentalized aspect of literacy. Information literacy is, in contrast, an inclusive term. Through information literacy, the other literacies can be achieved (Breivik, 1991). In attaining information literacy, students gain proficiency in inquiry as they learn to interpret and use information (Kuhlthau, 1987).

Defining Information Literacy

This early definition of information literacy evolved into a description of what it means to be information literate. The expanded definition focused on the attributes of one who is information literate. An information literate person is one who:

- recognizes that accurate and complete information is the basis for intelligent decision making

- recognizes the need for information

- formulates questions based on information needs

- identifies potential sources of information

- develops successful search strategies

- accesses sources of information including computer-based and other technologies

- evaluates information

- organizes information for practical application

- integrates new information into an existing body of knowledge

- uses information in critical thinking and problem solving (Doyle, 1992)

Applying Information Literacy

Not only has there been a significant increase in the amount of information available, but the rate at which that information becomes obsolete has increased as well. The area of "expertise" in which the average person can expect to keep current has grown proportionally smaller. The ability to sift through large amounts of information, and by making connections to prior knowledge, gain understanding, is a highly marketable skill. Those who know how to access and use information are likely to be more successful in a competitive marketplace.

In 1985, Sternberg expressed concern about the gap between a school's thinking skills curriculum and the application of thinking skills to real-life problem solving. He found that the first and most difficult step in problem solving was the ability to recognize that a problem exists and to define it. In a school curriculum, the problems are usually neatly labeled, while in the real world that almost never happens. In school lessons, clues are usually given by the teacher, or resources come in the form of prepackaged materials. In the real world, information searching strategies, using both print and non-print resources, must be learned and applied time and again. A final difference between school and real life lies in the solutions derived. In a classroom setting there is likely to be one correct solution. In real life experience, there are often many solutions, and alternatives must be weighed. The weighing process may include a search for further information, and it always involves placing the alternatives into a situational "real life" context.

Sternberg's identified gaps between the school and the real world can be bridged by applying the processes of information literacy: one must identify the problem, formulate a search strategy, acquire resources, and evaluate the information to determine whether it successfully solves the problem. Critical thinking and information literacy skills need to be consciously merged. They must become part of the assessment criteria for American students. While critical thinking skills provide the theoretical basis for the process, information literacy provides the skills for practical, real world application. Students need to acquire competence with critical thinking and information literacy skills in experiences that are part of the core curriculum. These experiences must simulate real life situations closely, because "real life" is what education purports to prepare students for. In so doing, cognitive research suggests that students will have a better mastery of the core curriculum as well. They will have made important connections between prior and new knowledge, (Caine & Caine, 1991) and learning will have greater meaning (Resnick & Klopfer, 1989).

In summary, the Information Age provides both opportunities and challenges for the future of education and the future of society. Managing large amounts of information, developing learning strategies to facilitate effective learning, and assuring that all citizens are skillful in the application of information are of critical importance. Information literacy, as a theme, provides a means to bring about the revolutionary changes called for by the evolutionary transitions in economics and education.

Chapter 1

Concept Evolution

While the evolution of a term is not important in and of itself, it often gives fuller meaning to a concept. The popularity of the Oxford English Dictionary attests to the value of concept development in historical definitions. This section combines an overview of the development of the term "information literacy" with a discussion of the larger field of national movements. These movements provide logical and political support for the development of information literacy as an organizing theme.

Early Use of the Term

The term "information literacy" was used in 1974 by Paul Zurkowski in a report to the National Commission on Libraries and Information Science. This report announced the establishment of a national program to achieve universal information literacy by 1984. Since 1974, many have worked long and hard to give substance and form to a concept that seemed intuitively correct.

Librarians have been especially sensitive to the information explosion and its resultant repercussions. The concept of information literacy, which advocates the preparation of people to be successful users of information, addresses librarians' concerns not only with the evolving nature of information sources and the overwhelming amount of information available, but also with the average user's lack of requisite information skills. Unfortunately, some library instruction is performing a disservice to the concept of information literacy by reducing the concept to an online catalog orientation. Librarians need to take care to connect the search for information to problem solving, to the real world, and to the practical use of information. The librarian's job is not completed with the finding of information. The information must be connected to the rest of the world in order for it to become knowledge. Several national movements point the way to this connection.

Development

A Nation at Risk (1983) identified the management of complex information in electronic and digital forms as an important skill in a "learning society." Surprisingly, this report made no recommendations on either the role of the library or of information resources in K-12 education. The National Commission on Libraries and Information Science (NCLIS), in response to the report, unanimously advocated "the importance of the role of library and information resources to underpin all learning and . . . the essential skills and proficiencies involved in finding and using information effectively. A basic objective of education is for each student to learn how to identify needed information, locate and organize it, and present it in a clear and persuasive manner" (Hashim, p.17).

NCLIS members, in the process of responding and developing strategy, agreed that a concept paper should be written to define what is meant by "information skills," as well as to identify the issues, questions, and problems related to the development of these skills. In "Educating Students to Think: The Role of the School Library Media Program" (Mancall, Aaron, & Walker, 1986), three relevant components of the school library media program were described. They were (1) the role of school library media programs in helping students develop thinking skills, (2) theoretical implications of current research on how children and adolescents process information and ideas, and (3) practical implications and applications of the concepts as a basis for developing an information skills program in all curricular areas.

Information Power

In 1988, the American Association of School Librarians (AASL), a branch of the American Library Association (ALA), published national guidelines for school library media programs. They called their work *Information Power*. These guidelines were significant in that they were developed using an innovative approach. First, the guidelines were developed in a joint effort with the Association for Educational Communications and Technology (AECT), another national professional organization with similar concerns. Secondly, the guidelines were stated in qualitative, rather than in quantitative terms. The vision presented in *Information Power* was of a school library media program that significantly expanded the access to and use of information and ideas by students, teachers, and parents.

The stated mission of *Information Power* is "to ensure that students and staff are effective users of ideas and information." This mission is accomplished by:

- providing intellectual and physical access to materials in all formats;

- providing instruction to foster competence and stimulate interest in reading, viewing, and using information and ideas; and

- working with other educators to design learning strategies to meet the needs of individual students (ALA, 1988).

Information Power called for a shift in the role of the library/media specialist from a passive "keeper of materials" to a key participant in the learning process. Today's library media specialists should be perceived as change agents in the restructuring of the educational process (Berkowitz & Eisenberg, 1988). Providing for a variety of resources as the basis for experiential learning, sharing with teachers the process by which students acquire needed information skills, and encouraging student pursuit of individual interests are all becoming accepted roles of the library media specialist.

Legitimization

As the concept of information literacy developed, an empirical and logical base needed to be identified. A major milestone in the development of the concept of information literacy was reached in 1987, when The Educational Resources Information Center (ERIC) published a monograph in which the term information literacy was an important part of the organizing structure. The monograph, *Information Skills for an Information Society: A Review of Research* (Kuhlthau, 1987) carved out a niche for information literacy—a base to which all could refer in the next stages of development and implementation.

In her monograph, Kuhlthau included library skills and computer literacy in the definition of information literacy. It is important to note that at this stage of development, library skills were described as "proficiency in inquiry" to correct the misconception that such skills are reserved only for the library. The library is an effective wellspring for these skills, but the larger focus is on student learning. Kuhlthau addressed two major themes in her monograph:

- Proficiency in inquiry for students is identified as the goal library media centers should set for integrating information literacy across curricular areas.

- Information technologies provide access to information resources that are critical to student learning. Computer literacy, once equated to computer operation, has been expanded to include the application and use of computers. Students use information technologies as tools in their search for appropriate information.

Kuhlthau's work pointed the way toward the integration of information literacy with curriculum, and presages the current development of the concept of information literacy with the library media center as the starting platform.

Formal Recommendations

In 1987, the American Library Association (ALA) president, Margaret Chisholm, appointed a Presidential Committee on Information Literacy. Membership in this blue ribbon committee included leaders in the fields of education and librarianship. Their final report, released in 1989, outlined six recommendations:

1. We all must reconsider the ways we have organized information institutionally, structured information access, and defined information's role in our lives at home, in the community, and in the work place.

2. A Coalition for Information Literacy should be formed under the leadership of the American Library Association, in coordination with other national organizations and agencies, to promote information literacy.

3. Research and demonstration projects related to information and its use need to be undertaken.

4. State Departments of Education, Commissions on Higher Education, and Academic Governing Boards should be responsible to ensure that a climate conducive to students' becoming information literate exists in their states and on their campuses.

5. Teacher education and performance expectations should be modified to include information literacy concerns.

6. An understanding of the relationship of information literacy to the themes of the White House Conference on Library and Information Services should be promoted (ALA, 1989, pp. 11-12).

The ALA policy statements and Kuhlthau's documentation in the literature set the stage for still further development. The subsequent level of interest in information literacy was illustrated by the deluge of requests

ALA received for their information literacy statement. There were three printings of the ALA report and nearly 20,000 were distributed. The ALA statement is powerful because it is written clearly and made forceful with concrete examples.

Dissemination

Based on the recommendation of ALA, a coalition for information literacy was "strategized" at an ALA sponsored meeting in April 1989, in Leesburg, Virginia. The first meeting of the National Forum on Informational Literacy (NFIL) took place on November 9, 1989, with Patricia Senn Breivik serving as chair. NFIL is a coalition of over 60 national organizations from business, government and education, all sharing an interest in and a concern for information literacy. NFIL has met quarterly since 1989 to promote the concept of information literacy as an imperative for the Information Age and to spread the concept to all professions.

NFIL is committed to fostering public awareness of the need for information literate people. Breivik summarized the coalition's activities in a 1990 progress report. The coalition is:

- identifying organizations whose purposes can be enhanced through the promotion of information literacy and inviting membership in or affiliation with the coalition;

- encouraging member organizations and individuals to advocate appropriate actions to promote information literacy;

- providing a national forum for the exchange of ideas and programs so as to create public awareness of the need for information literacy and to collect specific examples of how information literacy may affect individual Americans;

- developing a public awareness program using press releases, public service announcements, and other means to alert citizens to the importance of information literacy;

- monitoring emerging trends and patterns and encouraging research and demonstration projects; and

- promoting the establishment of a clearinghouse to gather and disseminate information on programs of information literacy and on efforts to promote information literacy.

NFIL member associations range widely. Included are representatives from the Information Industry Association, the National Conference of State Legislatures, the National Council of Teachers of English, the National Alliance of Black School Educators, several library groups, and an eclectic selection of other interested groups. Early meetings of NFIL focused on definitions and procedure. Gradually, supporting member associations included the topic of information literacy on their individual conference agendas. Dissemination from NFIL has been in the form of publications, especially in association journals and in-house newsletters from NFIL members.

In 1994, the American Association of School Librarians adopted national standards on information literacy based on *Information Literacy: A Position Paper on Information Problem-Solving*, (1993) developed by the Wisconsin Educational Media Association. These standards were endorsed by NFIL as well. These AASL standards outline seven basic elements in an information literacy curriculum:

- defining the need for information

- initiating the search strategy

- locating the resources

- accessing and comprehending the information

- interpreting the information

- communicating the information

- evaluating the product and process

The Association for Supervision and Curriculum Development (ASCD) has been represented in NFIL from the beginning. ASCD's resolutions for 1991 demonstrate commitment to the importance of information literacy (ASCD, 1991):

> Resolution #8, Information Literacy
> Today's information society transcends all political, social, and economic boundaries. The global nature of human interaction makes the ability to access and use information crucial. Differences in cultural orientation toward information and symbol systems make the management of information complex and challenging. Current and future reform efforts should address the rapidly changing nature of information and emerging information technologies. Information literacy, the ability to locate, process, and use information effectively, equips individuals to take advantage of the opportunities inherent in the global information society. Information literacy should be a part of every student's education experience.

The strategy of integrating the concept of information literacy into professional association activities has been rewardingly successful, and in turn, the associations have contributed to the dissemination of information in many different settings. For example, a current ERIC Digest on information literacy was written by the ASCD representative to NFIL (Hancock, 1993).

Accreditation

The Middle States Association of Colleges and Schools Commission on Higher Education has added an "assessment of information literacy in curriculum" to its agenda. The association's *Framework for Outcomes Assessment* uses the elements of information literacy:

> Of particular interest to Middle States is the extent to which students have mastered the ability to retrieve and use information. Most often, learning in this area begins with the courses offered in the general education program, and is refined as students move into more specialized curricula (1993).

Ralph A. Wolff (in press), Associate Executive Director of the Accrediting Commission for Senior colleges and Universities of the Western Association of Schools and Colleges echoes Middle States and adds: "Libraries can use the accrediting process as a vehicle for exploring the implications of new technologies and the goal of information literacy." The State University of New York Task Force on College Entry-Level Knowledge and Skills "recommends that teacher education and library school curricula incorporate strong information literacy components, so that all school teachers and librarians will be able to integrate information skills into their courses and other work with pupils." (SUNY, 1992).

While not directly related to accreditation, the American Association of Higher Education has an Action Community on Information Literacy, and sponsors the theme at each of its annual conferences. The National Education Association has been active in support of the concept as well. Initiatives by professional associations have a greater potential to effect long lasting change than any single advocacy, no matter how eloquent the spokesperson. The evolution of the concept of information literacy has been slow, but steady and lasting.

A Niche

In 1992, The ERIC System gave additional credence to the institutionalization of information literacy when it added the term to its descriptor listing. The director of the ERIC Clearinghouse on Information Resources, Dr. Michael B. Eisenberg, advocated the addition of this descriptor on the strength of increased requests to ERIC for information on the topic.

Chapter 2

Information Literacy in Context

For an innovation to be successful, it must be integrated into the fabric of existing professional practice. Some integrating approaches have been formal, such as the NFIL work, and other integrating approaches have been less formal such as the work done by individual advocates. Changes in education have been advanced at the national level as well. These changes include reform movements, restructuring approaches, alternative or more rigorous assessment practices, and the marketing of technology, among many others. Regardless of the intrinsic value of information literacy, it must develop in the milieu of larger social, economic, and political movements. The following review of how some of the more significant "change" movements are connected to information literacy provides some relational understanding. The connection these movements have with information literacy has great unifying potential.

Most major movements involve a confluence of events, ideas, and advocates. Two major events driving information literacy into the arena of ideas are the SCANS Report, *What Work Requires of Schools* (1991) and *Goals 2000*, also known as *America 2000*, the national agenda for education.

The SCANS Report

The SCANS Report outlined the economic shift in contemporary American society toward information services. It suggested and recommended skills that all Americans will need for entry level employment. These recommendations were phrased as outcome measures, and included both foundation skills and practical competencies. SCANS recommended a three-part skills foundation that included (1) basic skills, such as communication and understanding in reading, writing, and speaking; (2) thinking skills, such as problem solving, knowing how to learn, the generation of new ideas, setting goals, and choosing best alternatives; and (3) personal qualities, such as responsibility, self-esteem, sociability, self-management, and integrity and honesty (SCANS, p. xviii). There is a very close relationship between the full definition of information literacy and the recommendations of the SCANS Report. This congruency provides a powerful argument for advancing the concept of information literacy. When one looks at the five competencies outlined in the report, the argument becomes even stronger. These five competencies, the authors say, are necessary for all individuals entering the workplace: (1) identifies, organizes, plans, and allocates resources; (2) works with others; (3) acquires and uses information; (4) understands complex inter-relationships; and (5) works with a variety of technologies. While all five competencies conceivably relate to information literacy, number three directly addresses the issue. Let's look at competency (3) in detail.

Information: Acquires and uses information

- acquires and evaluates information

- organizes and maintains information

- interprets and communicates information

- uses computers to process information (SCANS, p. xvii)

Compare this to the expanded information literacy definition:

- recognizes that accurate and complete information is the basis for intelligent decision making

- recognizes the need for information

- formulates questions based on information needs

- identifies potential sources of information

- develops successful search strategies

- accesses sources of information including computer-based and other technologies

- evaluates information

- organizes information for practical application

- integrates new information into an existing body of knowledge

- uses information in critical thinking and problem solving

Once these competencies are achieved, students will have mastered the skills necessary for lifelong learning, and for providing information services to others "on-the-job." Students will have to learn how to acquire and organize information from sources that include the new information technologies. As they interpret and communicate their new understandings to others, they will demonstrate successfully their grasp of the three part foundation of education—basic skills, thinking skills, and personal qualities. This "purpose for schools" has been promoted by curricular reformers throughout the educational community.

At one time in American history, almost all students were trained for industrial types of employment. One cannot help but notice that there has been a pervasive and significant shift away from this notion. Now, all students need more than just the basic three R's to compete in the marketplace. They need to be able to think well, to communicate well, and to work effectively in groups. Schools are challenged to look beyond the immediate educational curriculum and to prepare students to be successful in the workplace. The traditional courses in literature, geography, and fine arts are still important, but classroom experiences must change. This does not mean that one needs to make college graduates out of all students. To think, to communicate, and to work cooperatively are skills every individual has always needed, but now these skills are crucial to the political, social and economic structure of the nation.

While information literacy is not explicitly mentioned in the SCANS Report, the five competencies mentioned in the report fit well with the comprehensive definition of the term. The extension of the three-part foundation beyond the 3 R's into listening/speaking skills and critical thinking skills, including knowing how to learn, imply skills that are included in the process of information literacy.

The primary setting for learning these skills and workplace competencies will still be the classroom, but there will be some drastic changes. Students will be encouraged from the start of their education to be self-directive, to work collaboratively with others, and to learn the process of information literacy which will assist them in problem solving and critical thinking. No longer will the traditional approach of the teacher as "sage on the stage" be appropriate. The role of the teacher will become "guide on the side," to facilitate students' learning. In the preparation of lifelong learners, assessments of success will be made by students as well as by teachers, and students will learn how to organize their own resources.

Today, a greater number of American students than ever have a secondary school education. In 1970, 75 percent of all students completed high school, compared with 33 percent in 1947. By 1990, the percentage of graduates was 83 percent—satisfactorily high, but 7 percent lower than the National Educational Goal of 90 percent (Richter, 1991). Despite these figures, forecasts of the labor market of the 21st century indicate large numbers of low-income, disadvantaged students are expected to drop out of school. This will be disastrous as it will occur at a time when more than half of new jobs will require education beyond high school (Darling-Hammond, 1990).

It is crucial that systemic changes be instituted now, so that all students will be prepared for employment. The shift to a service economy will require students to be prepared to work directly in information service jobs or be prepared to use information meaningfully in other jobs. The service industries will require employees who are able to adapt and learn new skills over the course of their careers—i.e. they must know how to learn. The value in advancing the concept of information literacy is that it applies to all settings, not just to those that are technology intensive.

The SCANS Report outlined an extensive reform program for education from a business perspective. The federal government developed a reform agenda for education also, and it fits closely with the SCANS Report in targeting needed changes.

National Education Goals

In February 1990, President Bush met with the National Governors' Conference in Charlottesville, Virginia, and together they announced the National Education Goals. Then Governor, Bill Clinton led the governors' task force in making the announcement. This marked the second time that national education goals had been established. In 1975, the National Governors' Conference publicized a list of national education goals, but little was done to implement them. In 1990 the goals were widely publicized by President Bush's administration. Under President Clinton, in 1994, legislation was passed authorizing *Goals 2000*, giving the goals legal status.

The aim of *Goals 2000* was expressed as: "individually, to promote higher levels of individual student achievement, and collectively, to build a globally competitive American work force" (*America 2000*, 1991, p. 2). Six goals were proposed, each having several subgoals that specified the issues to be addressed. Broadly, the six goals cover issues ranging from the education of preschool aged children to adult literacy. The underlying theme is the importance of lifelong learning, with particular emphases placed on schooling and preparation of students.

With *Goals 2000*, policy has been announced addressing diverse issues. Some of the goals, such as improvement of health and nutrition for preschool children, reduction of the dropout rate, and decrease in adult illiteracy, address social problems of contemporary America. Other goals include demonstrated competence in achievement and critical thinking skills, and achievement of world-class standing in math and science by the year 2000.

While the content of *Goals 2000* has remained as stated in the National Education Goals of 1990, there has been an important shift in emphasis, because the National Education Goals were policy statement, while *Goals 2000* was passed by Congress as federal legislation. While *America 2000* proposed 535 demonstration sites for exemplary practices, *Goals 2000* is committed to strengthening the public education system nation-wide (Congressional Digest, January 1994, p.8). The continuity of policy stems from its broad framework and the political reality that the leader of the Governors' Conference in 1990 was then Arkansas Governor, Bill Clinton. Thus, while President Bush adopted the goals as a national priority, his successor, having already vested in the development of the goals, took them a step further.

In brief form, the six goals as originally stated, are that, by the year 2000:

1. All children in America will start school ready to learn.

2. The high school graduation rate will increase to at least 90 percent.

3. American students will leave grades 4, 8, and 12 having demonstrated competency over challenging subject matter including English, mathematics, science, history and geography, and every school in America will ensure that all students learn to use their minds well, so that they may be prepared for responsible citizenship, further learning and productive employment in our modern economy.

4. U. S. students will be first in the world in mathematics and science achievement.

5. Every adult will be literate and will possess the knowledge and skills necessary to compete in a global economy and exercise the rights and responsibilities of citizenship.

6. Every school in America will be free of drugs and violence and will offer a disciplined environment conducive to learning.

In 1992, a national panel of experts from the organizational memberships comprising the National Forum for Information Literacy, collaborated in a Delphi study that looked at the National Education Goals. One objective of this panel was for them to specify the outcome measures of information literacy that could be correlated with the means for achieving selected National Education Goals. Success in reaching this objective would result in listing the ways in which these education goals could be attained by applying the process of information literacy. The National Education Goals were used as a framework to demonstrate the critical nature of information literacy in attaining information society goals. These goals would ultimately lead to successful education and employment for all Americans.

As a preliminary task, the group rated those education goals that members thought could be attained through information literacy skills. Goals 1, 3, and 5 were rated well above the others, and were the subjects for further consideration. The common theme of all three goals was life-long learning: children starting school ready to learn (Goal 1); students leaving grades 4, 8, and 12 demonstrating competency with subject matter and able to use their minds well (Goal 3); and all adults being literate and equipped with skills necessary to survive in the global economy (Goal 5).

Goal 1 stresses the pre-school, formative, affective aspects of developing a value for information. Goal 3, concerned with schooling, points to the attainment of skills necessary for successful living throughout life.

Goal 5 addresses the widespread application of skills to employment and citizenship. Since each goal pertains to a different age group, outcome measures differ, and each must be developmentally appropriate. The study demonstrated that information literacy skills are at the heart of successful attainment of these three goals.

Focus of Each Goal
Goal 1

Goal 1 calls for all children to start school ready to learn. The panelists agreed that this may be interpreted to mean that children should understand that the basic purpose of school is to allow them to acquire skills such as knowing how to learn, valuing information, and having a positive and enthusiastic attitude. Preschool children learn to value information by watching their parents, their first teachers. Other adults, including preschool teachers, are also role models. Motivation to read and access information begins with these first role models.

In order for children to start school ready to learn, a policy must include:

- a national commitment to the access of information for every American;

- community support through library facilities/community services for information rich resources, both print and non-print; and

- parents' acceptance of their responsibility to develop a value for information by reading to children and discussing what has been read.

Parents must value information and be able to demonstrate to their children effective strategies for accessing, evaluating, and using information. Many parents have yet to acquire these skills, so Goal 5, adult literacy, applies to them as learners. The continuum of lifelong learning is a circle. The present need for resources and skills development for adults affects future generations.

Goal 3

Goal 3 focuses on students learning how to use their minds well—knowing how to learn to make informed decisions. During the years of general education (K-12), all students need to learn how to process information as they apply problem solving and critical thinking skills to their school and personal lives. Learning these skills requires an active learning format where students process information to meet specific needs at a level that is developmentally appropriate. This inquiry approach is basic to active learning. An information rich environment is needed, where many resources are available including computer-based and other technologies. Teachers will need skills of their own to facilitate resource-based learning.

Comments by the panel members supported the notion that teachers are the most critical key to student attainment of information literacy. Because active learning represents a major shift in instructional strategy, a shift not often addressed in teacher preparation, extensive staff development programs will have to be conducted. Such staff development will have to be ongoing, over a period of years, as teachers build confidence and develop applications suitable for their own classes. Teachers must become information literate themselves, comfortable with a variety of resources, as well as with the process of accessing, evaluating, and using information. Assessments that integrate the process of information literacy into meaningful final projects, portfolios, or performances must be developed.

A library media center stocked with a wide variety of print and non-print resources was identified as critical to the integration of information literacy into the curriculum. Staffed with a trained library media specialist who collaborates with classroom teachers in carrying out classroom objectives, the library/media center should become the hub of a school, where equity of access to resources increases.

Sharing resources between school and community will become increasingly important. Rising costs and evolving technologies call for the rethinking of traditional institutions. References to no cost or low cost resources were thought to be misleading. There will always be costs to accessing information, and it must be determined at what point payment will be made. Equity of access must be guaranteed at the highest possible level (i.e. federal or state), or those who cannot pay for the opportunity to be knowledgeable will be penalized.

In order for students to become self-motivated, policy must include:

- National/state governments will make a commitment to ensure all students have equal and regular access to information by assuring adequate resources at each site.

- State Departments of Education/local school systems will develop and implement a resource-based learning curriculum.

- Curriculum standards that reflect a resource-based learning approach will be developed.

- Ongoing inservices will be conducted to ensure that teachers have the skills necessary to facilitate resource-based learning.

- Library/media centers will be recognized as key to successful implementation of resource-based learning.

- Parental support and participation in their children's learning will be considered integral.

- School goals will assure that information literacy skills are included across all curricular areas, so that all students apply information literacy as they learn the underlying principles of each curricular area.

- Sites will develop curricular objectives that include the process of information literacy across all curricular disciplines in the context of basic principles that are inherent to a particular subject area.

- Sites will develop curricular assessment methods that include alternative assessment procedures such as projects, portfolios, and performances involving the information literacy process.

- The library/media specialist will be an integral part of the instructional program, working in coordination with classroom teachers to carry out the curricular objectives.

- Teachers will implement resource-based learning in their classrooms.

- A variety of teaching strategies will be used to support students as active learners.

- Critical thinking/problem-solving skills will be developed and honed through meaningful activities involving the location and interpretation of information.

- Ongoing demonstrations will be made of how facts learned in classes become woven together to reveal the interrelated patterns of the world.

- Student assessment procedures will be used that include demonstration of the information literacy process, such as portfolios, projects, and performances.

- The library/media center will be viewed as an extension of the classroom (Doyle, 1992, pp. 5-6).

Goal 5

Goal 5 focuses on adult literacy and skills necessary for employment and citizenship. In terms of information literacy, all Americans need to be lifelong learners, able to access a variety of resources, proficient with various types of technologies, and able to evaluate and use information to meet personal and job-related needs. With over 80 percent of

American jobs somehow related to services, information has become the most important commodity in the marketplace. Those who can access information will be empowered with the skills necessary to be successful as employees and citizens.

The importance of addressing information literacy at the college level was recognized, although no specific outcome measures were suggested. Several panel members commented that this required immediate attention, so that college students can learn and/or reinforce information processing skills.

Panel members concluded that in order for all Americans to be lifelong learners, policy must state that:

- National/state governments will be actively involved in improving the information literacy of citizens.

- Communities will promote lifelong learning.

- Businesses will promote the acquisition of information literacy skills by all.

- All Americans will be able to seek information to solve problems and make informed decisions.

- A wide variety of print and non-print resources will be available to all Americans at no/low cost through public libraries, national online networks, and shared resources with business and public institutions.

- Colleges will recognize that information literacy skills must be mastered by all college graduates (Doyle, 1992, p.6).

Policy Implementation

The results of this research showed that the panel members reached consensus on 45 outcome measures for information literacy in the context of selected National Education Goals (*Goals 2000*). These results were in effect cross validated by the SCANS Report discussed earlier. There has been a rapid increase in public awareness concerning the need for information literacy skills, even though there may not yet be a conscious connection between the concept and the needed skills.

SCANS and *Goals 2000* are national policy statements, the latter having legal status. Still, it takes more than policy pronouncements to bring about the kind of change which will restructure the American educational system and produce students who are equipped for the Information Age. Both the SCANS Report and *Goals 2000* agree on much of what is needed: greater focus on teaching all students to become independent lifelong learners, to become critical thinkers, to use a variety of technologies proficiently, and to work effectively with others. Implicitly, all students must be prepared to use information literacy to solve problems in their personal lives as well as in the workplace. It is more important to know how to find needed information than to try to memorize and store facts for future reference.

Integrated change can often be brought about effectively by professional associations. National subject matter standards in several curricular areas have been revised recently. If the concept of information literacy is implied in these new standards, it needs to be drawn out and clearly identified.

An ERIC monograph, *Libraries for the National Educational Goals* (Stripling, 1992), shows the connection between quality library programs and effective implementation of the National Educational Goals. Each goal is reviewed and analyzed as to its library impact from the following perspectives: learning and schools, social context, and national values. Research efforts and model programs are outlined with impressive results. Libraries' role in achieving *Goals 2000* will be crucial for this national program to be successful.

Technology Impact

The educational reform reports of the 1980s were issued at the same time as personal computers and interactive technologies were established as important learning tools. From 1981 to 1987, U. S. public schools with at least one computer increased as follows: elementary schools, from 10 to 94 percent; junior high schools, from 15 to 98 percent; and senior high schools, from 41 to 99 percent (OTA, 1988).

Computers have been increasingly cited as important basic components of the instructional process. To date, the implementation of computers and related evolving technologies into instructional programs has been inconsistent. National technology policy statements that build a comprehensive vision have only recently emerged. As these policies are developed, they will help give direction to an effective implementation program.

Both the reform reports and the emergence of the new technologies during the 1980s pointed to an American economic transition that was occurring at the same time. Schools were seen as failing to turn out productive citizens and failing in their academic preparation of students. The needs of the American marketplace were changing from an industrial orientation to an information/service orientation. This change would lend impetus to a reform movement by the business community.

Power On! New Tools for Teaching and Learning, a report from the Office of Technology Assessment (OTA), was prepared at the request of the House Committee on Education and Labor of the U.S. Congress to study the benefits of interactive learning tools as improvers of the quality of education. The report also analyzed the technological, economic, and institutional barriers to achieving the technological competencies the future will require (OTA, 1988).

The report called for cooperative planning among all levels of governance, both to develop a plan and to share funding responsibilities. There was not a mandate for the federal government to assume a major role in prescribing the best solution, but rather a mandate to assure equity of access for all. Interactive technologies were identified as powerful and important tools for education, but a lack of comprehensive planning kept the technologies from achieving their potential. OTA has continued to lead in reporting progress in using technology in education.

Telecommunications offers all learners up-to-date information and continuous access to resources throughout the "global village." The Internet is a vast "virtual library," the library of the Information Age—but without an index or reference librarian to assist in finding appropriate materials. Developing the new electronic library is so essential, that a significant proportion of the $500 million contribution to education by the Walter H. Annenberg Foundation is designated for its creation. Schools preparing students to live in an information society are discovering that skills of empowerment for lifelong learning in this context require techniques similar to those librarians have been stressing for years, but with some important differences.

The process of information literacy requires not only the learning of a constellation of skills but also a new way of thinking in order to derive meaning from learning. Technological storage and sharing of information has increased the availability of data to an overwhelming volume. Much of this information is available only through telecommunications, and that proportion is growing rapidly. The ten criteria for information literacy apply to a larger area than telecommunications, yet telecommunications offers one an opportunity to examine the process.

Applying the Criteria

The process of acquiring information literacy is, to a large degree, facilitated by the new technologies, especially telecommunications. Here, then, is how the process of information literacy can work within the context of telecommunications.

Returning to the definition, an information literate person is one who:

- **recognizes accurate and complete information is the basis for intelligent decision-making**

- **recognizes the need for information**

These first criteria are affective, and they address the learner's values. Learners will have to realize they need accurate information in order to make informed decisions, and for many, this will involve basic attitude changes toward learning. Traditionally, students are taught to answer questions, and place value on a single right answer. How to ask the right question is not often taught. To motivate a student to take this new approach, one must take a constructivist approach and recognize the student's context. Questions will have to be meaningful to students and schools will be challenged to provide opportunities for students to explore "real life" needs for information. Connections between scholastic searches and personal problem solving will have to be made. This realistic approach is what motivates students. It is also where attitude changes.

- **formulates questions based on information needs**

As classrooms move from reliance on a single textbook for information to multiple sources in print and non-print formats, students will be encouraged to move away from finding the "right" answer (printed in a text), to finding the "best" answer from all available sources. Having decided that there is a need for information, learners will pose their need for that information in the form of a question. This is, probably, the most difficult part of all, and will call for critical thinking. The question, "What is it I really want to know?" must be answered clearly before one can decide where to search among resources. In this process the question may change as information emerges.

- **identifies potential sources of information**

There are thousands of information sources online including primary documents such as the federal budget or White House press briefings, experts with electronic mail (e-mail) addresses, and network computer servers with specialized information. Identifying potential sources of information will include online work for all learners. While teachers can provide background, they cannot teach searching by giving students books on computer based searches. The universe of available information is practically unlimited, although accessing it is tricky. Information literacy does not assume sources are easily identified. Indeed, in telecommunication networks, it can be very difficult to find a source, even if you know it exists. The process is akin to getting information in an oral culture where many questions must be asked before you find the person who has the knowledge you seek. Telecommunications gives the learner an efficient and a realistic search experience.

- **develops successful search strategies**

Developing search strategies has critical significance in telecommunications. In a study of "hits" in searching the PsychLIT database, fewer than 10 percent of university faculty and students used descriptors that matched PsychLIT terms (Thorngate & Hotta, 1990). The authors make the point that Aristotelian organization, the hierarchical classification of topics, only works when everyone classifies information in the same hierarchical way. Computer literacy is increasingly viewed as an enabling skill. It allows meaning to be extended and gathered from multiple resources. Computer literacy and information literacy are important skills to acquire, as are critical thinking skills. Computer literacy and information literacy are interrelated. Both types of literacy involve critical thinking, although acquiring computer literacy involves somewhat lower levels of skill in knowledge and understanding, as one learns how to use hardware and software (Cinque & Santomauro, 1987). Information literacy requires higher order skills that develop when the information collected is analyzed. To extend a metaphor, the electronic information space is not so much a highway as it is a landfill requiring considerable rooting and searching.

Online directories, changing constantly, may serve as pointers to resources, but sharing "finds" among users is still a top search strategy. Collaborative learning will be important. With the emergence of computer databases, sophisticated key word search strategies have been developed, and searching will take on a new look in this decade. Menu items on a gopher site may guide one into ERIC online searches, for example. Searchers will find a key word search and then prompts to help them continue on. This will move a searcher through a topic quickly, but will save time only if the searcher knows how to make proper use of descriptors. An important factor in computer searching is the fact that there will probably be midcourse corrections in search strategy based on the progress of the search. The rapid results one gets in electronic searching provide instant corrective information, not matched in traditional searching from printed sources. The searcher must know how to use these results and modify the search strategy accordingly. Most electronic card catalogue users quit after one try and may miss a great deal of useful information.

- **accesses sources of information including computer based technologies**

Libraries all over America find it increasingly difficult to maintain collections of up to date print materials. The cost of maintaining print collections is often prohibitive as funding is often low or non-existent. Technologies such as telecommunications give libraries "smart" alternatives. Telecommunications allows the library to receive information that's regularly updated, provides opportunities for searchers to ask experts to share their knowledge, and of course, allows unlimited numbers of comparatively easy searches. Educators must either help students develop competency in using technological tools, or see them forfeit the opportunity to become informed citizens and users of knowledge.

- **evaluates information**

Evaluating information is a skill that makes use of one's full range of critical thinking skills. Is the information accurate? Does the source provide verifiable evidence for the conclusions? Is the information current? Is it objective or subjective? Does the format—video, graphical, print, electronic—communicate clearly? Does the information answer the question being asked? An evaluation of the credentials of an electronic discussion group on medical problems, for example, showed that none of the participants held medical degrees, although all held authoritative appearing opinions and gave advice. All of the aforementioned must be taken into account as one critically evaluates information. As one uses a variety of resources, critical evaluation skills become increasingly important.

- **organizes information for practical application**

Organizing information also calls for critical thinking skills. The learner must answer questions such as "Have I found what I need? Are there gaps in my facts?" Organizing is also a communications step. Decisions regarding the format, the approach, and the intended audience are important in analyzing all information, even if the audience is the user alone. The information must be understandable, and must be organized in such a way that it can be recalled easily. With the large volume of information potentially obtainable using telecommunications, the organization of that information often requires the use of a computer database. This gives learners an opportunity to understand and experience the organizing of information. Understanding the usefulness of a database in organizing information can translate into real life skills for the student—how to maintain inventories in stores, for example.

- **integrates information into existing body of knowledge**

Learners demonstrate their comprehension of new information by integrating it into their existing personal storehouse of knowledge. This relates back to the original question the learner uses to guide the search. The learner evaluates what is already known in order to decide where new information is needed. What new information will bridge the gap between what is known and what needs to be known? Telecommunications provides almost instant access to an unsorted hodgepodge of elements. Merging those elements into useful information that can be integrated with existing knowledge is a skill that must be learned. Telecommunications offers a relatively easy way for the learner to "try on" different pieces of information, reject what "doesn't fit," and select the "best fit."

- **uses information in critical thinking and problem solving**

This criterion truly separates information literacy from mundane information seeking. The goal in information literacy is not to find information, a sort of academic scavenger hunt, but to do something practical with it. Once teachers thought written reports were the best way for students to demonstrate understanding, but an educational reform called "authentic assessment" suggests portfolios, projects, and products, are preferred ways for students to demonstrate understanding. Telecommunications skills—e-mail, downloading information from databases and gophers, conferring with subject experts, collecting and sharing scientific data with other students—can all be used to produce assessment products that can demonstrate understanding.

A restructuring of the instructional process is called for. Instead of teacher directed instruction, experience-based learning must become the norm in our schools. Information literacy is not concerned with the restructuring process in itself; however the new experience-based curricular design is of central importance in information literacy. One textbook expounded by the teacher must be replaced by a program that includes a variety of resources from which students extract needed information—in short, resource-based learning.

Resource-based learning is not the same as resource-based teaching. The latter refers to additional resources the teacher brings into the classroom to broaden instructional practices. The teacher makes all the decisions as to the appropriateness of materials. In resource-based learning, the students select the resources they think will best meet their needs for information. Their choices of materials may not differ from their teachers, but the focus has shifted to the students. Learning becomes an active, student-directed process. Students must learn how to learn (Haycock, 1991).

An Example of Resource-Based Learning

A statewide telecommunications project in California encourages student-directed learning. The Telemation Project focuses on developing curricular applications in K-12 learning environments using online resources. This curriculum project is encouraging a student centered learning approach based on California reform documents that emphasize a thinking-meaning curriculum. Twenty teachers, called Telementors, are developing instructional packages that integrate telecommunications with state curricular frameworks. When the packages are completed, the telementors will present five day workshops for other teachers in their region. They will also develop curricular projects to serve as models for other teachers who are ready to begin using telecommunications in their classrooms (Doyle, 1993).

Summary

Information literacy in telecommunications is achieved when learners know when to use online resources, know how to access information competently, know how to evaluate information as to accuracy and pertinence for each need, and know how to use this information to communicate effectively. Most of all, they have an opportunity to bring about change and be creative. Learners who are able to do this have a life long skill they will need in the Information Age.

Chapter 3

Assessment and Reform

To American educators, the term assessment usually equates with standardized testing, most typically the multiple choice, bubble-in variety. These norm referenced tests have become the accepted means for evaluating students for entrance into colleges, as well as for measuring academic achievement and intelligence. At their first strategy meeting in April 1989, the charter members of the National Forum for Information Literacy listed specific national measures for possible change. Inclusion of an "information literacy" assessment by Educational Testing Service was recognized as a lever for change in curricular emphasis. Assessment, and how it is done, is an important determinate of what constitutes curriculum.

Much of what is currently occurring in classrooms was first conceived in the early part of the twentieth century, during the industrial period of American economic history. School curriculum was viewed as a means for passing down to the student all the learning necessary for effective citizenry. The scientific management movement, translated into education, efficiently distilled out discrete facts and skills needing instruction (Isaksen & Parnes, 1985).

The American economy at that time was industrial. Educators preparing students to join the workforce identified competencies that "average" students should have to be a member of the semi-skilled employment pool. These skills included completing application forms, preparing shipping forms, and writing business letters (Wolf, Bixby, Glenn, & Gardner, 1991). More complex reasoning processes were reserved for students in "gifted" classes, who were assumed to be preparing to become the managers of the workforce.

As America began moving to a post-industrial, or information society, requisite skills for workers have taken a radical shift. A majority of the workforce needs skills that are technically oriented and that require judgment and conceptual understanding (Coates, Jarratt, & Malaffie, 1990). The ability to process information is integral to the emerging information society. Critical thinking skills, problem-solving skills, and competence in information literacy in order to process information are skills that must be acquired by all students.

Achievement of these important skills cannot be measured by testing discrete items. Many educational researchers are questioning the validity of norm referenced testing in the first place. Newer forms of assessment that view evaluation as an ongoing process include such measures as performance tasks, portfolio processes, and developmental assessment.

When learning is viewed as a process, assessment shifts to the achievement of criterion referenced objectives. This kind of assessment begins with the background each child brings to school, and ends with the competencies all high school graduates ought to possess. A baseline evaluation is made and regular assessment of developmental progress follows. A student's depth of understanding can be assessed, both by measuring incremental steps in developmental growth, and by looking at examples of actual experience in, for example, the critical thinking process involved in finding and evaluating information. Interestingly, resource-based learning approaches can help increase student performance on standardized norm-referenced tests as well. In *Information Literacy: Educating Children For the 21st Century* (in press), Breivik and Senn cite several examples where this has happened.

The multi-dimensional nature of finding and evaluating information can be separated and evaluated with criterion referenced measures. The process of the search strategy, from deciding the precise problem (stating the question), determining which resources to access, locating information, and finally, evaluating whether the accessed information best meets the need, can be included and measured in criterion referenced evaluation. Competence may be evaluated in the use of computers and computer related technologies, for example. Graduating high school students need skills in both areas as they prepare to join the contemporary workforce. It is a little difficult to see how the future of national assessment will fit with the concept of information literacy, because there are so many agendas to consider. That should not stop us from developing assessment measures for use at local levels, however.

The concept of educational reform is not new, of course, nor is the call for alternative assessment. In the mid-1950s, the launch of Sputnik stimulated the refocusing of American educational goals. Schools emphasized the academic and scientific aspects of education, and preparation of students for college became a prime national goal. The acquisition of theoretical knowledge by academicians and researchers became valued by society. An "information elite" emerged, consisting largely of those with skills in accessing and using information.

Traditionally, schools have not only been responsive to public policy, but they have also, on occasion, acted as instruments of the establishment. Consider the changes in the perceived value of schools in American society after more than two hundred years of history. In providing basic lessons for democracy, encouraging industrial development, and focusing on scientific research and technological development, schools have been instrumental in effecting the implementation of national policy. There has been a natural drift in the concept of assessment as curriculum evolved to meet the expectations of the public, at least as those expectations are understood by lawmakers. There have also been more focused efforts to bring about change. *A Nation at Risk* was one of the most publicized top down efforts. Other reports followed, and states often jumped onto reform "bandwagons," expending dollars from state income and sales tax revenues. The impetus for these reforms was the need, perceived by state governments, for improved schooling to encourage economic growth (Cuban, 1990).

The concept of educational reform has provided the impetus for change in educational practices to meet student and societal needs. Until 1990, when the Governors and the President assumed advocacy roles, no comprehensive program was in place to focus the needed sweeping changes. Now the challenge is to develop implementation policies that will truly direct the learning process. Information literacy must develop in the context of school reform, restructuring, assessment, and national goals. Such a challenge provides great opportunity, but also requires great effort and focus.

National Subject Matter Association Curriculum Standards

National policy statements declare the need for widespread reform and sound the alert for change in response to societal trends. In order for those changes, or new goals, to be attained, however, a mechanism must be established to define how and what changes are to made. Currently, the professional curricular organizations of major subject areas are engaged in the process of redefining their national standards. In this way, changes are emerging from the subject matter membership, rather than from legislative mandates. Past efforts to mandate change with federal and/or state initiatives have not been particularly successful, and the focus is now aimed at helping states, districts, and teachers establish their own standards within a framework of consistency.

Mathematics Standards

The National Council of Teachers of Mathematics (NCTM) paved the way for all national standards curriculum reform efforts. NCTM accomplished their task by asking for input, reaction, and buy-in from the widest possible audience of teachers and practitioners. The revision of mathematics standards took three years and included mailings to organizational memberships across the field of K-12 mathematics. A companion document concerning revision of teacher certification was also developed. Revising the K-12 mathematics curriculum required systemic changes in the "what" and "how" as well as the "who."

Curriculum and Evaluation Standards for School Mathematics (1989) views mathematics as "more than a collection of concepts and skills to be mastered; it includes methods of investigating and reasoning, means of communication, and notions of context. It involves the development of personal self-confidence" (NCTM, p. 5). Information literacy, as presented within this curriculum area, involves problem solving, the use of estimation, thinking strategies for basic facts, formulating and investigating questions from problem situations, use of computers, calculators, and other technologies.

Assessment of mathematics also fits within the larger picture of information literacy because the focus of evaluation is on using information in meaningful ways to demonstrate understanding.

Social Studies Standards

The National Council for Social Studies has been in the process of revising their standards for the past year and a half, with several steps yet to be completed before publication of *Curriculum Standards for the Social Studies* (1993). A second draft of their work is being reviewed by the Council's membership and the final version should be made available by the end of 1994. The social studies standards are grouped by school level (elementary, middle school, and high school), so that ten standards will be described and illustrated for each school level. Each level of a standard will include sidebars addressing related subjects, assessment samples, skills and values. In "Essential Skills for Social Studies," information literacy is integrated with achievement of the ten standards. While each standard lists the specific skills needed (or to be taught) to achieve understanding, the appendix lists all the essential skills together. "Skills Related to Acquiring Information," and "Skills Related to Organizing and Using Information" (Appendix A, pp. 88-89) are two of the three categories, and "Skills Related to Interpersonal Relationships and Social Participation" (Appendix A, p.89) is the third. The first two clearly parallel the process of acquiring information literacy.

To understand and apply the concepts covered in the social studies curriculum, all students will need practice in information literacy skills. The standards state that "it is important that students be able to connect knowledge, skills, and values to action as they engage in social inquiry." A responsibility and a privilege of democratic citizenship is the freedom to make difficult choices. Knowing how to locate and evaluate the facts that help one make informed choices is crucial. Helping students acquire the skills to make good decisions is the basis of the new social studies standards, and information literacy is implicitly and explicitly intertwined.

Science Standards

The National Committee on Science Education Standards and Assessment (NCSESA) of the National Research Council, first met in May 1992. Attending the meeting were representatives from the National Science Teachers Association, the American Association for the Advancement of Science, American Association of Physics Teachers, American Chemical Society, Council of State Science Supervisors, Earth Science Education Coalition, and the National Association of Biology Teachers. The group decided early on to integrate curriculum, teaching, and assessment standards into a single volume, so that each standard would reinforce the others, and produce a solid and complete vision for change. A preliminary draft of curriculum standards was released in February 1993. The final version should be published before the end of 1994.

The science standards, "Science for All," will include basic understandings of the physical, earth, and life sciences, divided into grade categories K-4, 5-8, and 9-12. There will also be sections on the "Nature of Science," "Applications of Science," and "Contexts of Science." It is in the sections on the "Nature of Science" and the "Applications of Science" that the process of information literacy becomes linked with successful learning.

The "Nature of Science" section includes "knowledge of the inquiry process, the ability to design and carry out an investigation, perspectives associated with critical thinking or habits of mind, and other positive attitudes usually associated with learning." The essential skills are those involved with conducting a scientific experiment and using critical thinking skills to analyze the results. This is an excellent application of information literacy using a hands-on approach appropriate to a particular subject matter. To be information literate, students must have experience in accessing, evaluating, and using information in different subject disciplines. It is the synthesis of these experiences that allows students to understand that critical thinking and decision making are important in all areas of life and that information literacy is the key that will open many doors.

The section of the science curriculum draft that deals with the "Applications of Science," addresses the use of appropriate scientific knowledge to "clarify and address issues and problems vital to informed decision-making in our society." As identified in these standards, decision making includes the ability to: formulate problem statements, identify dimensions of an issue, gather information, generate and evaluate alternative solutions, recommend a preferred solution, participate in decision-making, and understand decision-making. The development of decision making skills in students requires that they have guided practice and experience in all areas of the curriculum, and the study of science offers special insights and contributions in this regard. The development of these skills in the science context is complimentary to the development of these skills in the information literacy context. This type of cross-disciplinary theme building is rewarding for all involved.

Performance Standards—A Common Vision

The Forum on Standards and Learning was created in February 1994 to address issues that cut across, and extend beyond standards now being developed in respective subject areas. The Forum is co-sponsored by the College Board and six national subject-matter organizations—the National Council of Teachers of Mathematics, the National Council of Teachers of English, the National Science Teachers Association, the National Council for the Social Studies, the Music Educators National Conference, and the American Council on the Teaching of Foreign Languages. Together, these associations represent more than 280,000 teachers and educators nationwide as well as several thousand secondary and postsecondary institutions across the country. The Forum seeks to ensure that standards will contribute to a common vision of learning and, at the same time, be regarded as living documents, never entirely finished, but always open to the potential for improvement and change (correspondence from the Forum on Standards and Learning to the National Education Goals Panel, March 3, 1994).

Content and performance standards alone, however, without information literacy, i.e., without preparing citizens to know when information is needed, to know how to identify, locate, evaluate, and effectively use information to deal with any issue or problem at hand, will not produce the skills all Americans will need for lifelong learning and problem solving in the real world. This is the issue that advisory groups and national organizations concerned with national subject standards need to address.

Concluding Remarks

In the past decade, information literacy has enjoyed increasing amounts of attention as a concept at the heart of the development of independent lifelong learners. As American society has shifted from an economy based on capital goods (industrial) to an economy based on services (information), there has been a corresponding shift in what is expected from American education. Recent research in how learning occurs has shown this shift in the focus of American education to be realistic and educationally sound. Knowing how to ask the right questions may be the single most important step in learning. The process that is conducted in order to find answers to the right questions leads to the point at which information becomes knowledge. It is at this point where facts are internalized into personal meaning by the learner. Information literacy—the ability to access, evaluate, and use information from a variety of sources—is central to all successful learning and by extension to all successful living.

The challenge of education is to develop creative and rational thinkers who can solve problems and who can be reflective (Costa, 1985; Marzano, 1988; Resnick & Klopfer, 1989). Teachers' skills must be directed to designing complex and appropriate experiences for learners.

Allowing students to make connections and process information so that they will be able to derive their own conclusions is of critical importance to all successful learning experiences (Caine & Caine, 1991). Research into cognitive processes has shown clearly that personal experience, the discovery of meaning, and the discerning of connections, are necessary conditions for successful learning. Students learn best when they connect new experiences with older ones, and then extend the connection to new possibilities. This requires thinking! As students prepare for the 21st century, the traditional basic courses in reading, mathematics, and writing needs to be coupled with communication, critical thinking, and problem solving skills. (Costa, 1985). Information literacy is the platform upon which these skills can stand, consisting as it does of knowledge of resources and tools of access, skillful search strategies, and appropriate techniques of processing information (Kuhlthau, 1987).

There is a great deal of work yet to be done. The concept of information literacy is still being developed. Many more examples of how information literacy can shape and be integrated into curriculum are needed. The work of incorporating information literacy abilities into the subject specific standards of national organizations needs to be continued. Further research into the effect of resource-based learning on students' academic and career performance needs to be conducted. The curriculum in many colleges of teacher education will have to be changed to reflect the inclusion of information literacy standards. The best demonstration of applications for learning information literacy will be found in the classroom. The best demonstration of the results of an information literate population will be found in the citizenship and economic well being of the nation.

References

American Association of School Librarians and Association for Educational Communications and Technology. (1988). *Information power: Guidelines for school library media programs.* Chicago: Author. (ED 315 028)

American Library Association Presidential Committee on Information Literacy. Final Report. (1989). Chicago: Author. (ED 316 074)

Association for Supervision and Curriculum Development, Resolutions. (1991). Alexandria, VA: ASCD.

Berkowitz, R. E., & Eisenberg, M. B. (1988). The library media specialist and information literacy. *New York Secondary Schools Board Association Journal, 20,* 17-18, 21.

Breivik, P. S. (1991). A signal for the need to restructure the learning process. *NASSP Bulletin, 75*(535), 1-7. (EJ 425 568)

Breivik, P. S. & Senn, J. A. (in press). *Information literacy: Educating children for the 21st century.* NY: Scholastic.

Caine, R. N., & Caine, G. (1991). *Making connections: Teaching and the human brain.* Alexandria, VA: ASCD. (ED 335 141)

Cinque, H. & Santomauro, D. (1987). *Information literacy: Application, software, and critical thinking. An experience and a proposal.* Paper presented at the National Educational Computing Conference. Dallas, TX. (ED 308 878)

Coates, J. F., Jarratt, J., & Malaffie, J. B. (1990). *Future work: Seven critical forces reshaping work and the work force in North America.* San Francisco: Jossey-Bass.

Costa, A. L. (Ed.) (1985). *Developing minds: A resource book for teaching thinking.* Alexandria, VA: ASCD. (ED 262 968)

Cuban, L. (1990). Four stories about national goals for American education. *Phi Delta Kappan, 72*(4), 264-271. (EJ 418 152)

Darling-Hammond, L. (1990). Achieving our goals: Superficial or structural reforms? *Phi Delta Kappan, 72*(4), 286-295. (EJ 418 155)

Doyle, C. S. (1992). *Final report to National Forum on Information Literacy.* Syracuse, NY: ERIC Clearinghouse on Information Resources. (ED 351 033)

Doyle, C. S. (1993). *Telemation Project Executive Summary.* Seal Beach, CA: California State University, California Technology Project.

Hashim, E. (1986). Educating students to think: The role of the school library media program, an introduction. In Information literacy: Learning how to learn. A collection of articles from *School Library Media Quarterly, Journal of the American Association of School Librarians, 17.* Chicago: ALA 1991.

Hancock, V. E. (1993). *Information literacy for lifelong learning.* An ERIC Digest. Syracuse, NY: ERIC Clearinghouse on Information Resources. (ED 358 870)

Haycock, C. A. (1991). Resource-based learning: A shift in the roles of teacher, learner. *NASSP Bulletin, 75*(530), 15-20. (EJ 425 570)

Isaksen, S. G., & Parnes, S. J. (1985). Curriculum planning for creative thinking and problem solving. *Journal of Creative Behavior, 19*(1), 1-29. (EJ 319 929)

Kuhlthau, C. C. (1987). *Information skills for an information society: A review of research.* Syracuse, NY: ERIC Clearinghouse on Information Resources. (ED 297 740)

Mancall, J. C., Aaron, S. L., & Walker, S. A. (1986). Educating students to think: The role of the library media program. A concept paper written for the National Commission on Libraries and Information Science. *School Library Media Quarterly, Journal of the American Association of School Librarians, 15*(1), 18-27. (EJ 344 239)

Marzano, R. J. (Ed.) (1988). *Dimensions of thinking: A framework for curriculum and instruction.* Alexandria, VA: ASCD. (ED 294 222)

Middle States Association of Colleges and Schools. Commission on Higher Education. (1993). *Framework for outcomes assessment.* Baltimore, MD: Author.

National Commission of Excellence in Education. (1983). *A Nation at risk: The imperative for educational reform.* Washington, DC: U.S. Government Printing Office. (ED 226 006)

National Council for the Social Studies. (1993). *Curriculum standards for the social studies, draft 2.* Washington, DC: NCSS.

National Council of Teachers of Mathematics. Commission on standards for school mathematics. (1989). *Curriculum and Evaluation Standards for School Mathematics.* Reston, VA: NCTM. (ED 304 336)

National Research Council. (1993). *National science education standards: An enhanced sampler. A working paper of the National Council on Science Education Standards and Assessment.* Washington, DC: NRC. (ED 360 175)

Office of Technology Assessment. (1988). *Power on! New tools for teaching and learning: Summary.* Washington, DC: U.S. Government Printing Office. (ED 295 677)

Resnick, L. B., & Klopfer, L. E. (1989). *Toward the thinking curriculum: Current cognitive research.* Reprinted. Alexandria, VA: ASCD. (ED 328 871)

Richter, P. (1991, Oct.1). Students held lacking in hi-tech skills. *Los Angeles Times.* A16.

Secretary's Commission on Achieving Necessary Skills. (1991). *What work requires of schools: A SCANS report for America 2000.* Washington, DC: U.S. Government Printing Office. (ED 332 054)

State University of New York. (1992). *SUNY 2000. College expectations: The report of the SUNY task force on college entry-level knowledge and skills.*

Sternberg, R. (1985). Teaching critical thinking, Part I: Are we making critical mistakes? *Phi Delta Kappan, 67*(3), 194-98. (EJ 327 970)

Stripling, B.K. (1992). *Libraries for the National Education Goals.* Syracuse, NY: ERIC Clearinghouse on Information Resources. (ED 345 752)

Staff. (1994, January). Goals 2000 and America 2000. *Congressional Digest, 73*(1), 8.

Thorngate, W. & Hotta, M. (1990). Expertise and information retrieval. *Knowledge: Creation, Diffusion, Utilization. 11*, 237-247.

U. S. Department of Education. (1991). *America 2000: An educational strategy. Source book.* (ED 327 985)

Wisconsin Educational Media Association. (1993). *Information literacy: A position paper on information problem-solving.* Appleton, WI: WEMA Publications.

Wolf, D., Bixby, J., Glenn, J., & Gardner, H. (1991). To use their minds well: investigating new forms of student assessment. In G. Grant (Ed.) *Review of research in education* (No.17). Washington, DC: American Educational Research Association.

Wolff, Ralph A. (in press). Rethinking library self studies and accreditation visits. In Ralph A. Wolff, *The challenge and practice of academic accreditation: A sourcebook for library administrators*. New York, NY: Greenwood Press.

Wurman, M. (1989). *Information anxiety.* NJ: Doubleday.

Zurkowski, P. G. (1974). The information service environment relationships and priorities. Related paper no. 5. *National Commission on Libraries and Information Science.* (ED 100 391)

Annotated ERIC Bibliography

Periodicals

Adams, S. & Bailey, G. D. (1993). Education for the Information Age: Is it time to trade vehicles? *NASSP Bulletin, 77*(553), 57-63. (EJ 463 900)

Traditional instruction employs a text/talk vehicle focused on basic literacy, with little effort to engage students in information literacy, or accessing, analyzing, synthesizing, applying, and creating information with electronic media. This article provides the Information Age Teaching-Learning Audit to help principals assess their schools' progress in understanding and using emerging instructional technologies such as computers, CD-ROMs, videodiscs, scanners, e-mail, and other audiovisual aids.

Baldwin, K. (1992). Information skills in the primary classroom. *Reading, 26*(3), 25-30. (EJ 462 216)

Observes primary children's information skills and identifies areas of difficulty. Discussion of modifying and developing such skills through specific teaching methods focuses on the case of one student whose response to gathering information from difficult text was to copy the text word for word.

Breivik, P. S. (1991). Literacy in an information society. *Community, Technical, and Junior College Journal, 61*(6), 28-29, 32-35. (EJ 428 980)

Today's definition of literacy must include the ability to find and evaluate needed information. Proposes a national literacy agenda to change the way information is used in educational settings and provide greater access to expanding information resources. Considers information literacy a means of personal and national empowerment.

Breivik, P. S. (1991). A signal for the need to restructure the learning process. *NASSP Bulletin, 75*(535), 1-7. (EJ 425 568)

Although the U.S. will not disintegrate tomorrow if information literacy and resource-based learning remain underfunded, today's disadvantaged groups will fall further behind, as a new "information elite" emerges. The American Library Association's 1989 information literacy report is one step toward creating a national agenda for improving everyone's information access.

Breivik, P. S. (1992). Education for the Information Age. *New Directions for Higher Education, 20*(2), 5-13. (EJ 450 248)

To be effective in the current rapidly changing environment, individuals need more than a knowledge base. They also need information literacy which includes techniques for exploring new information, synthesizing it, and using it in practical ways. Undergraduate education should focus on such resource-based learning directed at problem solving.

Breivik, P. S. & Ford, B. J. (1993). Promoting learning in libraries through information literacy. *American Libraries, 24*(1), 98, 101-02. (EJ 457 956)

Discusses information literacy and describes activities under the sponsorship of the National Forum on Information Literacy (NFIL) that promotes information literacy in schools and libraries. Activities of member organizations of the NFIL are described, including policy formation, publications, and programs; and the role of the American Library Association (ALA) is explained.

Breivik, P. S. & Jones, D. L. (1993). Information literacy: Liberal education for the Information Age. *Liberal Education, 79*(1), 24-29. (EJ 464 246)

The challenge for higher education today is to develop better ways to guide individuals through rapidly expanding old and new resources in their search for knowledge. This means helping undergraduates develop skills in information literacy, the effective seeking and packaging of information.

Breivik, P. S. & Shaw, W. (1989). Libraries prepare for an Information Age. *Educational Record, 70*(1), 12-19. (EJ 387 384)

Since funding levels will probably not change much, college libraries will need to shift emphasis from seeking more funding for current and new services to delivering more and better service for less, becoming leaner and more able to deliver adaptable services. Increased budget flexibility will be essential.

Cuban, L. (1990). Four stories about national goals for American education. *Phi Delta Kappan 72*(4), 264-71. (EJ 418 152)

Presents four versions of American educational history highlighting centralization/decentralization issues, American faith in schooling, and cascading national and international changes requiring extraordinary reforms. These diverse stories all arrive at the same conclusion--a need for national goals and performance standards to guide policy makers.

Curran, C. (1990). Information literacy and the public librarian. *Public Libraries, 29*(6), 349-53. (EJ 421 649)

Describes the current concept of information literacy as a survival skill and suggests that public libraries can play an important role in its spread if they develop some nontraditional practices and make alliances with other agencies.

Darling-Hammond, L. (1990). Achieving our goals: Superficial or structural reforms? *Phi Delta Kappan 72*(4), 286-95. (EJ 418 155)

President Bush and the nation's governors have proposed that by 2000, all children will leave grades 4, 8, and 12 with demonstrated competency in challenging subject matter and use of their minds. This article discusses the improvements needed in curriculum and testing, teachers and teaching, and school superstructures.

Dimitroff, A. et al. (1990). Alliance for information: Michigan librarians and library faculty join forces for the future. *Research Strategies, 8*(2), 52-58. (EJ 416 997)

Describes a cooperative program between the library school and university library at the University of Michigan which addresses information literacy and information in a diverse society. The discussion covers program-related courses on information resources and American diversity; the library/library school relationship; and management issues including the role of librarians, incentives, and academic governance.

Eisenberg, M. B. & Berkowitz, R. E. (1992). Information problem-solving: The Big Six Skills approach. *School Library Media Activities Monthly, 8*(5), 27-29, 37, 42. (EJ 438 023)

Explains the components of a library and information skills curriculum and integrated instructional model that was developed to help students solve information problems. The six steps include (1) task definition, (2) information seeking strategies, (3) location and access, (4) use of information, (5) synthesis, and (6) evaluation.

Eisenberg, M. B. & Brown, M. K. (1992). Current themes regarding library and information skills instruction: Research supporting and research lacking. *School Library Media Quarterly, 20*(2), 103-10. (EJ 441 731)

Reviews research that addresses four major themes about library and information skills instruction in library media programs: (1)

the value of library and information skills instruction; (2) the content of library and information skills; (3) teaching library skills in the context of subject area curriculum; and (4) alternative methods for teaching library media skills.

Eisenberg, M. B. & Small, R. V. (1993). Information-based education: An investigation of the nature and role of information attributes in education. *Information Processing and Management, 29*(2), 263-75. (EJ 462 841)

Describes the concept of Information Based Education, provides a theoretical basis for investigating the role of information in education, and develops a classification scheme for documenting and distinguishing among information bases. Attributes of information associated with information resources, information skills, information transfer, technology, content, and instruction are presented.

Eisenberg, M. B. & Spitzer, K. L. (1991). Skills and strategies for helping students become more effective information users. *Catholic Library World, 63*(2), 115-20. (EJ 465 828)

Addresses the implications for education of the expansion of information technology and proposes a model for teaching information skills within the context of an overall process. The "Big Six Skills" model is presented, and its application to information problems related to school, life, and work is explained.

Farmer, D. W. (1992). Information literacy: Overcoming barriers to implementation. *New Directions for Higher Education 20*(2), 103-12. (EJ 450 258)

Fundamental attitudinal and behavioral changes must occur among faculty, librarians, and students before colleges can implement effective information literacy programs. Successful change will require acknowledgment of barriers, collaborative effort, and establishment of a learning community for an information-rich environment.

Goodin, M. E. (1991). The transferability of library research skills from high school to college. *School Library Media Quarterly, 20*(1), 33-41. (EJ 436 241)

Describes a study designed to determine whether a program of instruction to teach high school students information-gathering skills would prove useful to them in college. Results indicate that the program has a significant impact on students' attitudes and performance, but whether the skills transfer to undergraduate studies is unclear.

Haycock, C. (1991). Resource-based learning: A shift in the roles of teacher, learner. *NASSP Bulletin, 75*(535), 15-22. (EJ 425 570)

The ability to process and use information effectively is not only an empowerment tool for students, but a basic survival skill. To develop information in students means that schools must legitimize the teaching and learning process. Teachers must function as facilitators of learning in collaboration with students, other teachers, and library media specialists.

Huston, M. M., (Ed.). (1991). Toward information literacy--Innovative perspectives for the 1990s. *Library Trends, 39*(3), 187-362. (EJ 431 616)

This issue contains 12 articles that present library perspectives on information literacy. Topics discussed include critical thinking and bibliographic instruction (BI); learning style theory and reference desk interviews; teaching information retrieval to end users; library instruction for faculty; cognitive authority; question formulation techniques; and BI for users with diverse cultural backgrounds.

If we had information standards, what would they be? Information and library media skills documents. (1994). *School Library Media Activities Monthly, 10*(5), 49-50. (IR 528 003)

Discussion of the development of educational standards and the impact on school library media programs focuses on what constitutes information skills, or information literacy. Documents for 27 states are listed that outline the information skills actually taught in the various states.

Irving, A. (1992). Information skills across the curriculum. *School Library Media Annual (SLMA), 10,* 38-45. (EJ 454 760)

Discusses the need to incorporate information skills across the curriculum. Problems facing school libraries are examined; strategies to promote information skills across the curriculum are suggested; the use of information technology is considered; examples of current practice in the United Kingdom are described; and implications for librarians are addressed.

Isaksen, S. G. & Parnes, S. J. (1985). Curriculum planning for creative thinking and problem solving. *Journal of Creative Behavior 19*(1), 1-29. (EJ 319 929)

Reports results of a survey of 150 curriculum planners about their knowledge, attitudes, and behavior regarding deliberate development of creative thinking and problem-solving skills. A six-step creative problem-solving model is proposed.

Lenox, M. F. & Walker, M. L. (1993). Information literacy in the educational process. *Educational Forum, 57*(3), 312-24. (EJ 465 008)

To prepare information-literate citizens, teachers should (1) shift focus from product to process; (2) recognize and accommodate diverse styles of learning information; (3) integrate information seeking into learner-based curriculum; and (4) help students understand the view of information as a commodity and the issues surrounding access.

Mancall, J. C. et al. (1986). Educating students to think: The role of the school library media program. *School Library Media Quarterly 15*(1), 18-27. (EJ 344 239)

Discusses recommendations from the National Commission on Libraries and Information Science for defining, developing, and promoting library media programs that teach information finding and using skills. Areas covered include helping students develop thinking skills, theoretical implications of current research on how children process information, and applications in curriculum development.

McGovern, J. (1990). A plan for integrating information and thinking skills into the curriculum. *School Library Media Activities Monthly, 6*(5), 26-29. (EJ 405 616)

Describes six lessons developed by a library media specialist and two fifth-grade teachers that integrate information skills and content with thinking skills to provide a meaningful research context for students. For each lesson, the specific information and thinking skills targeted, learning activities, resources used, and evaluation methods are outlined.

Ross, S. L. (1990). Information skills in the information laboratory. *School Library Media Activities Monthly, 6*(7), 31-33. (EJ 407 239)

Describes a process approach to library media skills instruction which would focus on the development of students' critical thinking skills and give them the ability to examine and utilize information. The importance of instructing students in database searching and ways that database searching will enhance information skills development are also addressed.

Stanford, L. M. (1992). An academician's journey into information literacy. *New Directions for Higher Education, 20*(2), 37-43. (EJ 450 251)

For one college teacher, the experience of reading "Information Literacy; Revolution in the Library" revealed a new and informative pattern in learning and teaching. This article examines information literacy and instructional development, classroom application, and student services.

Sternberg, R. J. (1985). Teaching critical thinking, Part 1: Are we making critical mistakes? *Phi Delta Kappan 67*(3), 194-98. (EJ 327 970)

Describes the significant differences between the kinds of problems that adults really face and the problems that students are taught to resolve in critical thinking programs. Among the differences are several aspects of the ways in which problems and solutions are defined.

Turner, P. M. (1991). Information skills and instructional consulting: A synergy? *School Library Media Quarterly, 20*(1), 13-18. (EJ 436 238)

Argues that the school library media specialist's instructional consultation role can optimize the impact of information skills, and proposes that the choice of the information skills be dictated by (1) the cognitive requirements of the lesson; (2) the teacher's instructional design decisions; and (3) the learning characteristics of the students.

Werrell, E. L. & Wesley, T. L. (1990). Promoting information literacy through a faculty workshop. *Research Strategies, 8*(4), 172-80. (EJ 423 342)

Discusses information literacy and describes a faculty development workshop designed to provide a forum for improving library research assignments. Faculty impact on students' information use and critical thinking skills is discussed, characteristics of effective research assignments are described, and course-integrated library research is discussed.

Wesley, T. (1991). Teaching library research: Are we preparing students for effective information use? *Emergency Librarian, 18*(3), 23-24, 26-30. (EJ 423 325)

Discussion of using library instruction to teach a decision-making process focuses on the importance of teaching students how to use information rather than just how to find it. Highlights include planning a research strategy, topic analysis, consideration of relevant perspectives, choice of appropriate information sources, and evaluating information sources.

ERIC Documents

American Association of School Librarians and Association for Educational Communications and Technology. (1988). *Information Power: Guidelines for school library media programs*. Chicago: Author, 185 pp. (ED 315 028)

Developed jointly by the American Association of School Librarians (AASL) and the Association for Educational Communications and Technology (AECT), these guidelines for the school library media specialist are based on the premise that teachers, principals, and library media specialists must form a partnership and must plan together to design and implement the program that best matches the instructional needs of the school. Emphasis is placed on the responsibility of the building level media specialist to exercise leadership in establishing the partnerships and initiating the planning process. The central unifying concept of the guidelines is the provision of both physical and intellectual access to information, increasingly through networks extending well beyond the school. The guidelines are presented in eight chapters: (1) The Mission and the Challenges; (2) The School Library Media Program; (3) The School Library Media Specialist: Roles and Responsibilities; (4) Leadership, Planning, and Management; (5) Personnel; (6) Resources and Equipment; (7) Facilities; and (8) District, Regional, and State Leadership. Seven appendixes provide: a report on a survey of school library media centers; budget formulas for materials and equipment; library media facility guidelines; policies and statements on access to information; a list of selected research studies; and lists of individuals who have contributed to the development of the guidelines, either financially or as professional consultants. An annotated bibliography lists 12 sources of information on the history of school libraries and six guides to national standards and guidelines for school library media programs published between 1920 and 1975.

American Library Association Presidential Committee on Information Literacy. Final report. (1989). Chicago, IL: American Library Association, 21 pp. (ED 315 074)

This discussion of information literacy as a tool for achieving professional and personal goals argues that information literacy for individuals is a means of becoming empowered, i.e., being able to find and make sense of information to refute or verify expert opinion, without being utterly dependent on others for information. The value of being information literate in business is demonstrated through examples of losses or near losses to businesses that did not know how to find or use information effectively. Information literacy is also defined as a central element in the practice of democracy, with responsibilities on both the side of the government to make information available, and on the side of citizens to make use of the information as part of political decision making. A new model for education is suggested, based on the information resources of the real world (e.g., online databases, videotapes, government documents, and journals), and on learning that is active and integrated rather than passive and fragmented. The dynamics of an information age school are also discussed. Six recommendations for actions that would enable the United States to reap the benefits of the Information Age conclude the report.

Burnheim, R. (1992). *Information literacy: The keystone of the bridge.* Paper presented at the TAFE National Conference on Student Services (Brisbane, Australia, October 14-16, 1992), 15 pp. (ED 356 775)

This paper discusses information literacy skills and procedures for breaking information resources into their component data. The paper draws on the work of two Australian committees to establish the importance of these skills and briefly describes a research project on library services required to support the delivery of competency-based training curriculum. Structures and strategies for breaking information into component parts and recombining those parts are identified, and a list of information competencies developed by Michael Marland is included. The concluding section suggests that librarians and teachers should work together to provide students with materials and activities that will enable them to develop information skills. Four charts that can be used for information retrieval are appended.

Caine, R. N. & Caine, G. (1991). *Making connections: Teaching and the human brain.* Alexandria, VA: Association for Supervision and Curriculum Development, 201 pp. (ED 335 141)

This book adds to the growing body of knowledge and research suggesting that educators need to move beyond simplistic, narrow approaches to teaching and learning. In Part I, "Accessing the Brain's Potential," current educational practices are examined in light of critical findings of brain researchers. In Part II, "Facts and Theories about the Human Brain," topics, theories, and models of brain functions that seem to address current issues in education and provide implications for curriculum restructuring and design are considered. Major aspects of research are reorganized for the purpose of eliciting a useful and practical set of general principles. In Part III, "Brain-Based Schooling," elements of instruction that are believed to cause students to use the brain's capacity more fully to learn are discussed.

California Media and Library Educators Association. (1994). *From library skills to information literacy: A handbook for the 21st century.* Castle Rock, CO: HiWillow, 167 pp. (IR 054 998)

This book is a guide for those making the change from a traditional library media center or classroom to one based on the new information literacy. Highlights include models and strategies that encourage children and young adults to find, analyze, create, and use information. Numerous scenarios and sample lessons assist those involved in local planning. Appendixes include a report on integrating literacy into national agendas and also as a planning guide to research process competencies.

Cinque, H. A. & Santomauro, D. J. (1987). *Information literacy: Application software and critical thinking. An experience and a proposal.* Paper presented at the National Educational Computing Conference (Dallas, TX, June 15-17, 1988), 18 pp. (ED 308 878)

This paper describes the development of a course to introduce microcomputer application software to non-computer science majors at Kean College (New Jersey). Topics covered include: (1) background; (2) course content; (3) classroom laboratory design, installation, and management; (4) teaching strategies and student performance and reactions. Some related conceptual issues are then discussed, and a proposal for offering computer literacy as a general education course is presented. The paper concludes with discussions of computer literacy, the rationale for incorporating critical thinking skills in the curriculum, the relationship between application software and critical thinking, and problems with considering the course as a general education offering. (21 references)

Costa, A. L., (Ed.). (1985). *Developing minds: A resource book for teaching thinking.* Alexandria, VA: Association for Supervision and Curriculum Development, 347 pp. (ED 262 968)

This 10-part resource book contains 54 articles which address topics related to helping students become effective thinkers. The articles are organized under these categories: (1) the need to teach students to think; (2) creating school conditions for thinking; (3) definitions of thinking (including goals for a critical thinking curriculum); (4) a curriculum for thinking; (5) how thinking pervades the curriculum; (6) teacher behaviors that enable student thinking; (7) teaching strategies intended to develop student thinking; (8) programs for teaching thinking (providing criteria for examining any curriculum to enhance intelligent functioning, describing many of the major programs designed to develop the intellect, identifying the audience for whom each program is intended, and distinguishing among the several theoretical and philosophical assumptions on which each is based); (9) computers and thinking; and (10) assessing growth in thinking abilities. Additional articles are presented which provide resources for teaching thinking. Other resources (in

10 appendices) include a glossary of cognitive terminology, questions for system planners, overhead transparency masters, and various checklists and observation forms.

Doyle, C. S. (1992). *Outcome measures for information literacy within the National Education Goals of 1990. Final report to National Forum on Information Literacy. Summary of findings.* 18 pp. (ED 351 033)

This report summarizes the findings of a study that was conducted for the National Forum on Information Literacy (NFIL), a group of representatives from 46 national organizations from business, government, and education which share an interest and concern with information literacy. The purpose of this study was to create a comprehensive definition of information literacy and to develop outcome measures for the concept. The National Education Goals of 1990 were used as a framework to demonstrate the critical nature of information literacy for attainment of selected goals. The study employed the Delphi research technique, through which a panel of 56 selected experts were assisted to reach consensus on the definition and the outcomes. This report presents the concise definition of information literacy formulated by the panel--i.e., the ability to access, evaluate, and use information from a variety of sources--as well as a listing of 10 discrete attributes of an information literate person. Of the six National Education Goals of 1990, three that the panel ranked as relevant to the desired outcomes of information literacy are then discussed: (1) all children should start school ready to learn; (2) elementary and secondary school students need to learn how to learn in order to make informed decisions; and (3) adults must be provided with the literacy and other skills necessary for employment and citizenship. It is noted that these goals represent a continuum for lifelong learning, and the panel's recommendations for specific policies at the national, state, and local levels to facilitate these outcomes are listed for each goal. Appendices provide lists of the members of the panel of experts who completed the project, the organizations represented in the study, and the items upon which the panel achieved consensus.

Eisenberg, M. B. & Berkowitz, R. E. (1990). *Information problem solving: The Big Six Skills Approach to library and information skills instruction.* Norwood, NJ: Ablex (ED 330 364). Document Not Available from EDRS.

This book presents a systematic approach to integrated library and information skills instruction that is based on six broad skill areas necessary for successful information problem-solving, otherwise referred to as the "Big Six Skills." It begins with definitions and explanations of the Big Six Skills approach, moves to a discussion of implementation, and concludes with specific exemplary instructional units and lessons. Six chapters emphasize practical and tested techniques to develop and implement library and information skills instructional programs based on the Big Six Skills approach: Chapter 1 revisits the overarching concepts and themes of the approach; chapter 2 defines and explains an expanded view of the specific levels of the Big Six Skills; chapter 3 provides contextual examples and exercises to develop a better understanding of the Big Six Skills; chapter 4 focuses on practical actions that relate to planning and implementation of the approach; chapter 5 offers exemplary instructional units to act as models for elementary and secondary settings; and chapter 6 provides examples of generic lessons that can be adapted to assist in delivering the desired integrated instruction. Two appendixes include completed exercises from chapter 3 and four sample curriculum maps generated from a K-12 sample curriculum database. A subject index and a 27-item bibliography are also provided.

Eisenberg, M. B. & Berkowitz, R. E. (1988). *Resource companion for curriculum initiative: An agenda and strategy for library media programs.* Norwood, NJ: Ablex (ED 307 890). Document Not Available from EDRS.

This resource book is intended as a companion to the book "Curriculum Initiative: An Agenda and Strategy for Library Media Programs," which provides practicing school library media specialists and students in professional degree-granting programs with both a conceptual framework and practical approaches to the curriculum-related responsibilities of the school library media program. It is divided into two major parts: worksheets and tools, and graphic masters. Within each part, the materials are organized by section, and each section focuses on a particular task, area, or concept. Part I comprises worksheets and tools designed to assist in carrying out the information gathering, assessment, and design of activities outlined in the Six-Stage Strategy, which was presented in the companion to this book. The tools are divided into six logical, interrelated sections: (1) curriculum mapping; (2) curriculum support services; (3) curriculum planning; (4) instruction; (5) assessment; and (6) time management. Part II is composed of a series of visuals developed to assist in presenting and promoting the agenda and strategy proposed in the earlier work, and is divided into four interrelated sections: (1) curriculum support services; (2) the Big Six Skills; (3) general management concepts and tools; and (4) the Six-Stage Strategy. The visuals are intended for use as masters for overhead transparencies and handouts to enhance presentations to all constituencies relevant to the library media program, i.e., teachers, administrators, students, library media professional and support staff, boards of education, school and district committees, and various community groups. An 11-item bibliography is provided.

Gardner, D. P. et al. (1983). *A nation at risk: The imperative for educational reform. An open letter to the American people. A report to the nation and the Secretary of Education.* Washington, DC: National Commission on Excellence in Education, 72 pp. (ED 226 006).

This report: (1) investigates the declining state of the educational system in America, as measured by high school student performance in the United States and other countries; (2) identifies specific problem areas; and (3) offers multiple recommendations for improvement. The five major recommendations arrived at appear, respectively, under the headings: content, standards and expectations, time, teaching, leadership and fiscal support. Recommendations pertaining to content include the strengthening of high school graduation requirements by establishing minimum requirements for each student of: (a) 4 years of English; (b) 3 years of mathematics; (c) 3 years of science; (d) 3 years of social studies; and (e) one-half year of computer science. With regard to standards and expectations, schools, colleges, and universities are encouraged to adopt more rigorous and measurable standards and higher expectations for academic performance and student conduct. Four-year colleges and universities, in particular, are advised to raise their admission requirements. In order to improve time usage, the report advises that more time should be devoted to students learning the "New Basics," which may, in turn, require a longer school day, or a lengthened school year. Seven ways to improve teacher preparation and to make teaching a more rewarding and respected profession are listed. Six implementation guidelines are suggested for improving educational leadership and fiscal support. Appendices contain: (a) charter of the National Commission on Excellence in Education; (b) schedule of the Commission's public events; (c) list of commissioned papers; (d) list of individuals who testified at Commission hearings; (e) list of other presentations to the Commission; and (f) notable programs.

Hancock, V. E. (1993). *Information literacy for lifelong learning. ERIC Digest.* Syracuse, NY: ERIC Clearinghouse on Information Resources, 4 pp. (ED 358 870)

Information literacy requires that the learner recognize the need for information, be able to identify and locate it, gain access to it, and then evaluate the quality of the information received before organizing it and using it effectively. In an information literate environment students engage in active and self-directed activities. Information literacy thrives in a resource-based learning environment in which students and teachers make decisions about appropriate sources of information and how to access them. Information literacy benefits students by counteracting the information dependency created by traditional schooling and sets the teacher free to become the facilitator of interaction at the small-group or individual level. Information literate students are more effective consumers of information resources, and become better-prepared citizens, who know how to use information to their best advantage in work and everyday life. The workplace of the future will also demand information literate workers. An early commitment to learning as a process will enable the worker of the future to function effectively.

Jay, M. E. et al. (1988). *Information power: Guidelines for school library media programs. A discussion guide.* Chicago, IL: American Association of School Librarians & Washington, DC: Association for Educational Communications and Technology, 28 pp. (ED 315 029)

The most recent set of national guidelines for the development of school library media programs, which was published in 1988, identifies underlying changes in the roles of the school library media specialist as well as in the program itself. Viewing the library media specialist as an initiator of curricular activities rather than a purveyor of support services, these guidelines emphasize leadership, partnership, planning, curricular needs, collection development, and equity of access to information. This discussion guide has been developed to help educators at all levels to plan meetings and conduct effective discussion sessions with persons who have become familiar with "Information Power" in its entirety, in order to evaluate local school library media programs in light of the recent revisions. The first of three sections identifies the principal concepts presented in "Information Power" and provides an overview of each of its eight chapters. Procedures by which discussion sections may be effectively organized to promote the successful exchange of knowledge and views are recommended in the second section. The final section identifies specific constituencies for discussion groups and suggests discussion questions for each of the groups--i.e., library media specialists, administrators and boards of education, classroom teachers, college and university faculty, state department of education personnel, and members of the community at large--as well as questions for mixed constituency groups and questions basic to all discussion sessions.

Kuhlthau, C. C. (1987). *Information skills for an information society: A review of research. An ERIC Information Analysis Product.* Syracuse, NY: ERIC Clearinghouse on Information Resources, 34 pp. (ED 297 740)

This review of the research literature describes and discusses functional/information literacy in the age of computers and the resulting "information explosion," together with means by which students can become competent information users in the future and be enabled to lead productive, meaningful lives. Defined as comprising library skills and computer literacy, information literacy is discussed in relationship to school media centers, which have become key places for integrating skills and resources with subjects across the curriculum, and allowing students to develop proficiency in inquiry. This study summarizes information technologies useful in schools and reviews international information literacy programs to provide insights into ways that administrators, teachers, and library media specialists can work together to prepare students to meet the challenges of the Information Age. Included in the discussion are (1) definitions and characteristics of information literacy; (2) the library media center as information center; (3) integrating information skills with the curriculum; (4) information technologies in schools; and (5) means of achieving information literacy. It is concluded that competent use of information can offer beneficial results to society-at-large, and that, conversely, information illiteracy can cause harm to individuals and to society.

Lowe, M. T. (1993). *Cooperative planning and information access skills.* 59 pp. (ED 359 974)

To determine if cooperative planning between the library media specialist (LMS) and the classroom teacher affects the integration of information access skills into the curriculum, classroom teachers in grades 1 through 5 were surveyed in 10 randomly selected schools in Cobb County (Georgia). Of the 183 teachers surveyed, 131 returned questionnaires, a response rate of 72 percent. Classroom teachers (60.3 percent) stated that the LMS influenced their teaching of information access skills by providing resources either through classroom visitations or in planning sessions. Classroom teachers reported that topics of instruction during cooperative planning were discussion of useful materials and the examination of materials. Through cooperative planning, teachers stated, the introduction of information sources by the LMS helped them teach information access skills. Discussing and previewing resource materials and defining objectives appeared to be the primary areas of school LMS influence. Eleven tables present study data, and appendixes contain the cover letter and the 16-item survey questionnaire.

Marzano, R. J. et al. (1988). *Dimensions of thinking: A framework for curriculum and instruction.* Alexandria, VA: Association for Supervision and Curriculum Development, 175 pp. (ED 294 222)

Organizing and clarifying research and theory from diverse sources, including philosophy and cognitive psychology, this book provides a framework intended to help educational practitioners (principals, supervisors, curriculum directors, and teachers) plan programs for incorporating the teaching of thinking throughout the regular curriculum. Chapter 1 discusses the need for a framework for teaching thinking and presents a historical perspective on the study of thinking. Chapters 2 through 6 discuss five dimensions of thinking: (1) metacognition; (2) critical and creative thinking; (3) thinking processes--such as concept formation, problem solving, and research; (4) core thinking skills--the "building blocks" of thinking--including focusing, information-gathering, organizing and generating skills; and (5) the relationship of content-area knowledge to thinking. The final chapter presents guidelines for using the framework. (A glossary of key terms and an outline of the book are appended, and thirteen pages of references are attached.)

National Research Council-National Academy of Sciences. (1993). *National science education standards: An enhanced sampler. A working paper of the National Committee on Science Education Standards and Assessment.* Washington, DC: NRC, 91 pp. (ED 360 175)

The National Research Council is coordinating the development of national standards for science education in grades K through 12. By the fall of 1994, National Science Education Standards will be completed and published. The standards will contain narrative descriptions of what all students should be able to do to engage and understand the natural world. The standards will address science curriculum, teaching, and assessment and will represent the consensus of teachers and other science educators, scientists, and the general public. The following chapters are included; (1) "Introduction"; (2) "Taking Up the Challenge"; (3) "A Framework for the Content Standards"; (4) "Fundamental Understandings and Prototype Standards for the Physical Sciences"; (5) "Fundamental Understandings for the Life Sciences"; (6) "Nature of Science"; (7) "Application of Science"; and (8) "Context of Science."

Office of Technology Assessment. (1988). *Power On! New tools for teaching and learning: Summary.* Washington, DC: U.S. Government Printing Office, 263 pp. (ED 295 677)

This report on the potential of new interactive technologies for improving learning examines developments in the use of computer-based technologies, analyzes key trends in hardware and software development, evaluates the capability of technology to improve learning in many areas, and explores ways to substantially increase student access to technology. The role of the teacher, teachers' needs for training, and the impact of federal support for educational technology research and development are reviewed as well. Specific topics addressed include the adoption of computer and video technologies; evaluation research; computer-assisted instruction (CAI) and intelligent CAI; mathematics and science; multimedia programs; database management; word processing; language arts; electronic networks; cost-effectiveness; software; and research and development. The future of classroom instruction is discussed in terms of networking and distance education, CD-ROM and computer/video convergence, hypermedia, integrated learning systems, and videodisks. Appended materials include a summary of state activities in educational technology; criteria used to evaluate educational software; principal programs of the U.S. Department of Education that are providing funds for technology in education; a list of acronyms; and a bibliography of contractor reports. Also included are a copy of the September 1988 OTA Report Brief entitled "Power On! New Tools for Teaching and Learning," and a September 15, 1988 Press Release announcing two videotapes on the influence and potential of educational technology in public schools, now available from SL Publications, New York.

Resnick, L. B., Ed. & Klopfer, L. E., (Ed.). (1989). *Toward the thinking curriculum: Current cognitive research. 1989 ASCD Yearbook.* Alexandria, VA: Association for Supervision and Curriculum Development, 231 pp. (ED 328 871)

A project of the Center for the Study of Learning at the University of Pittsburgh, this yearbook combines the two major trends/concerns impacting the future of educational development for the next decade: knowledge and thinking. The yearbook comprises the following chapters: (1) "Toward the Thinking Curriculum: An Overview" (Lauren B. Resnick and Leopold E. Klopfer); (2) "Instruction for Self-Regulated Reading" (Annemarie Sullivan Palincsar and Ann L. Brown); (3) "Improving Practice through Understanding Reading" (Isabel L. Beck); (4) "Teaching Mathematics Concepts" (Rochelle G. Kaplan and others); (5) "Teaching Mathematical Thinking and Problem Solving" (Alan H. Schoenfeld); (6) "Research on Writing: Building a Cognitive and Social Understanding of Composing" (Glynda Ann Hull); (7) "Teaching Science for Understanding" (James A. Minstrell); (8) "Research on Teaching Scientific Thinking: Implications for Computer-Based Instruction" (Jill H. Larkin and Ruth W. Chabay); and (9) "A Perspective on Cognitive Research and Its Implications for Instruction" (John D. Bransford and Nancy J. Vye).

Stripling, B. K. (1992). *Libraries for the National Education Goals.* Syracuse, NY: ERIC Clearinghouse on Information Resources, 125 pp. (ED 345 752)

Focusing on the major educational initiatives of our times--the National Education Goals outlined and endorsed in 1990 by the nation's governors, and President Bush's America 2000 strategy--this report reviews and summarizes information about the role of libraries in many different educational efforts designed to meet the national goals. It is argued that libraries can and must play a pivotal role in meeting these goals, including efforts to prepare students to cope with learning in an information age (resource-based learning), and to provide a national electronic network for students, teachers, administrators, and community members (the National Education and Research Network). This work provides direct evidence of the relationship between existing and developing library programs and the national education initiatives, citing specific examples whenever possible or appropriate. A separate chapter is devoted to each of the six goals to be reached by the year 2000. Within each chapter, information is presented for each of three spheres of influence defined in "Education Counts: An Indicator System To Monitor the Nation's Educational Health" (U.S. Department of Education, 1991)--learning and schools, social context, and national values. Within each sphere of influence, examples of ways in which libraries can contribute to meeting the goal are presented together with research findings, comments, and highlights of programs already involved in the types of activities related to a particular example, and sources of the information given are cited. A 15-item selected bibliography of sources on which this work is based concludes the report.

Todd, R. et al. (1991). *Evolution, not revolution: Working to full school participation with information skills.* Paper presented at the Biennial Meeting of the Australian School Library Association (Levra, New South Wales, Australia, September 29-October 3, 1991) 19 pp. (ED 354 909)

An action research project underway at Marist Sisters' College, a secondary school in New South Wales, is the first phase in the evolution of an across-the-school commitment to Cooperative Program Planning and Teaching (CPPT). Project goals include establishing an infrastructure to develop a dynamic methodology for CPPT in the school; facilitating the achievement of the individual teacher's goals for CPPT; and widening the CPPT base in the school to establish a school-wide commitment to information skills. To establish an infrastructure, a school-based interdisciplinary management team was formed. The team identified characteristics of the school, teachers, and administrative staff that could act as catalysts and change agents. Barriers to program development were identified. Understanding the attitudes of teachers toward information skills was a necessary step prior to development of the project planning model. The model was applied to a year 7 science unit, in order to demonstrate the teacher's use of the CPPT approach. The program emphasizes the dynamic role of the teacher-librarian as a teaching partner and change agent for educational innovation.

Todd, R. J. et al. (1992). *The power of information literacy: Unity of education and resources for the 21st century*. Paper presented at the Annual Meeting of the International Association of School Librarianship (21st, Belfast, Northern Ireland, United Kingdom, July 19-24, 1992), 22 pp. (ED 354 916)

Information literacy is the ability to use information purposefully and effectively. It is a holistic, interactive learning process encompassing the skills-based phases of defining, locating, selecting, organizing, presenting, and evaluating information from sources that include books and other media, experiences, and people; being able to consider information in light of knowledge; adding information to current knowledge; and applying this knowledge to solve information needs. An approach for promoting information literacy and establishing an integrated information skills program in a school is described. At Marist Sisters' College, a secondary school in Sydney (Australia), an action research project has attempted to place information literacy at the center of the curriculum. Using R. G. Havelock's model of the change agent, a range of change agent activities has been used. Qualitative evaluation through interviews with 8 teachers and 110 students in grades 7, 9, and 11 has demonstrated the positive impacts of the approach on student self-concept, the learning process, the view of information, learning outcomes, and the learning environment. Three appendixes contain a summary of the information process, change agent activities, and a diagram of the planning model.

U.S. Department of Education. (1991). *America 2000: An education strategy. Sourcebook.* Washington, DC, 89 pp. (ED 327 985)

"America 2000" is a long-term national strategy (not a federal program) designed to accomplish in nine years (by the year 2000) the six national education goals articulated by the President and the state governors at the 1989 "Education Summit" in Charlottesville, Virginia. This national education strategy was presented by the President in a ceremony at the White House on April 18, 1991, and a booklet describing the basic features of the strategy was published at that time (see ED 327 009 for document and an abstract summarizing the strategy). This "Sourcebook" is, in its own words, "a collection of documents that together offer a comprehensive description of America 2000." It contains: (1) remarks by the President at the presentation of the national education strategy (April 18, 1991); (2) the full contents of the original booklet articulating the details of the four parts of the strategy, including a glossary of key terms and "some questions and answers"; (3) the White House fact sheet or press release summarizing the strategy; (4) the six national education goals to be attained by the strategy; and (5) the joint statement by the President and state governors made September 27-28, 1989 at the "Education Summit."

U. S. Department of Labor. Secretary's Commission on Achieving Necessary Skills. (1991). *What work requires of schools. A SCANS report for America 2000.* Washington, DC: U. S. Government Printing Office, 60 pp. (ED 332 054)

The Secretary's Commission on Achieving Necessary Skills (SCANS) examined the demands of the workplace and whether young people were capable of meeting those demands. Specifically, SCANS determined the level of skills required to enter employment. Fundamental changes in the nature of work were identified; these changes were found to hold implications for the kinds of workers and workplaces the nation must create. The research verified that "workplace know-how" defined effective job performance. This know-how had two elements: competencies and foundation skills. To describe how this know-how is used on the job, five scenarios were developed that portray work requirements in the context of the real world. The scenarios came from five sectors of the economy: manufacturing, health services, retail trade, accommodations and food service, and office services. They showed that work involved a complex interplay among five competencies (resources, interpersonal, information, systems, and technology) and three elements of the foundation (basic skills, thinking skills, and personal qualities). A proficiency scale with five levels was proposed: preparatory, work-ready, intermediate, advanced, and specialist. Three major conclusions were reached: (1) all U.S. high school students must develop the competencies and foundation skills; (2) the high performance qualities of the most competitive companies must become the standard for most companies; and (3) the nation's schools must become high performance organizations. (A letter to parents, employers, and educators and an executive summary are provided. Appendixes include definitions of the competencies and the foundation.)

Zurkowski, P. G. (1974). *The information service environment relationships and priorities. Related paper no. 5.* National Commission on Libraries and Information Science. Washington, DC: National Program for Library and Information Services, 30 pp. (ED 100 391)

The relations of the National Program for Library and Information Services to information literacy and the information industry are discussed. Private sector information resources are identified in several categories. The traditional relations of libraries and with the information industry are described, and examples are given of situation where traditional roles of libraries and private sector information activities are in transition. It is suggested that the top priority of the National Commission on Libraries and Information Science should be directed toward establishing a major national program to achieve universal information literacy by 1984.

How to Order ERIC Documents and Article Photocopies

Documents

Individual copies of most ERIC documents (ED numbers) are available in either microfiche or paper copy from the ERIC Document Reproduction Service, 7420 Fullerton Road, Suite 110, Springfield, VA 22153-2852; some are available only in microfiche. Information needed for ordering includes the ED number, the number of pages, the number of copies wanted, the unit price, and the total unit cost. Sales tax should be included on orders from Maryland, Virginia, and Washington, DC.

The prices of paper copy are based on units of 25 pages (and/or any fraction thereof) at the rate of $3.53 per unit. The prices for microfiche are based on the number of microfiche for each document. The price for one to five microfiche for a single document is $1.23 (up to 480 pages) plus $.25 for each additional microfiche (96 pages for that document).

Shipping charges for microfiche via first class mail begin at $.52 for one to seven fiche and $.75 for 8-19 fiche; add postage for an additional ounce for each additional ten or eleven microfiche up to a total of 80. Documents and orders for more than 80 microfiche are shipped via UPS in the continental United States, and charges should not exceed $3.77 for one pound (81-160 microfiche or 1-75 pages). Estimate one pound for each additional 170 microfiche or 75 pages of paper copy.

For additional information about ordering call 1-800-443-3742 or 703-440-1400.

Journal Articles

Copies of journal articles (EJ numbers) are not included in the ERIC Microfiche Collection. Photocopies of articles from many of the journals indexed by ERIC are available from the UMI Article Clearinghouse, 300 N. Zeeb Rd., Ann Arbor, MI 48106. Information needed for ordering includes the author, title of article, name of journal, volume, issue number, page numbers, date, and EJ number for each article. The price is $12.50 for each article and must be prepaid. Additional copies of the same article are $2.50 each, up to 50 copies. (Lower prices are available to deposit account customers.) For additional information, call UMI at 1-800-521-0600 ext. 2533, 2534, or 2786.